Contents

VELVEETA Ultimate Queso Dip

Prep: 5 min. ● Total: 10 min.

1 lb. (16 oz.) **VELVEETA** Pasteurized Prepared Cheese Product, cut into ½-inch cubes

1 can (10 oz.) RO*TEL® Diced Tomatoes & Green Chilies, undrained

MIX VELVEETA and tomatoes in microwaveable bowl.

MICROWAVE on HIGH 5 min. or until **VELVEETA** is completely melted, stirring after 3 min.

SERVE with tortilla chips or assorted cut-up vegetables.

Makes 3 cups or 24 servings, 2 Tbsp. each.

SIZE-WISE:

When eating appetizers at social occasions, preview your choices and decide which you'd like to try instead of taking some of each.

CREATIVE LEFTOVERS:

Cover and refrigerate any leftover dip. Reheat and serve over hot baked potatoes or cooked pasta.

SUBSTITUTE:

Prepare as directed, using VELVEETA Mild Mexican Pasteurized Prepared Cheese Product with Jalapeño Peppers.

*Ro*Tel® is a product of ConAgra Foods, Inc.*

VELVEETA Chili Dip

Prep: 5 min. • Total: 10 min.

1 lb. (16 oz.) **VELVEETA** Pasteurized Prepared Cheese Product, cut into
   ½-inch cubes

1 can (15 oz.) chili with or without beans

MIX VELVEETA and chili in microwaveable bowl. Microwave on HIGH 5 min.
or until **VELVEETA** is completely melted and mixture is well blended, stirring
after 3 min.

SERVE hot with tortilla chips, toasted chips or assorted cut-up vegetables.

Makes 3 cups or 24 servings, 2 Tbsp. each.

HEALTHY LIVING:

Save 20 calories and 2 grams of fat per serving by preparing with VELVEETA Made
With 2% Milk Reduced Fat Pasteurized Prepared Cheese Product.

HOW TO HALVE:

Mix ½ lb. (8 oz.) VELVEETA Pasteurized Prepared Cheese Product, cut up, and ¾ cup
canned chili in 1-qt. microwaveable bowl. Microwave on HIGH 3 to 4 min. or until
VELVEETA is melted, stirring after 2 min. Serve as directed. Makes 1¼ cups or
10 servings, 2 Tbsp. each.

TO SERVE A CROWD:

Mix 1½ lb. (24 oz.) VELVEETA Pasteurized Prepared Cheese Product, cut up, and 2 cups
canned chili in 2½-qt microwaveable bowl on HIGH 4 min.; stir. Microwave 4 to 6 min.
or until VELVEETA is melted, stirring every 2 min.; stir. Serve as directed. Makes 5 cups
or 40 servings, 2 Tbsp. each.

Hot Broccoli Dip

Prep: 30 min. • Total: 30 min.

1 loaf (1½ lb.) round sourdough bread

½ cup chopped celery

½ cup chopped red bell peppers

¼ cup chopped onions

2 Tbsp. butter or margarine

1 lb. (16 oz.) **VELVEETA** Pasteurized Prepared Cheese Product, cut into ½-inch cubes

1 pkg. (10 oz.) frozen chopped broccoli, thawed, drained

¼ tsp. dried rosemary leaves, crushed

Few drops hot pepper sauce

PREHEAT oven to 350°F. Cut slice from top of bread loaf; remove center, leaving 1-inch-thick shell. Cut removed bread into bite-sized pieces. Cover shell with top of bread; place on baking sheet with bread pieces. Bake 15 min. Cool slightly.

MEANWHILE, cook and stir celery, red bell peppers and onions in butter in medium saucepan on medium heat until tender. Reduce heat to low. Add **VELVEETA**; cook until melted, stirring frequently. Add broccoli, rosemary and hot pepper sauce; mix well. Cook until heated through, stirring constantly.

SPOON into bread loaf. Serve hot with toasted bread pieces, crackers and/or assorted cut-up vegetables.

Makes 2½ cups or 20 servings, 2 Tbsp. each.

USE YOUR MICROWAVE:

Mix celery, red bell peppers, onions and butter in 2-qt. microwaveable bowl. Microwave on HIGH 1 min. Add VELVEETA, broccoli, rosemary and hot pepper sauce; mix well. Microwave 5 to 6 min. or until VELVEETA is melted, stirring after 3 min.

VARIATION:

Omit bread loaf. Spoon dip into serving bowl. Serve with crackers and assorted cut-up vegetables as directed.

SUBSTITUTE:

Prepare as directed, using VELVEETA Made With 2% Milk Reduced Fat Pasteurized Prepared Cheese Product.

Crowd-Pleasing Recipes

Crispy Tostadas

Prep: 10 min. • Total: 17 min.

- 8 tostada shells (5 inch)
- 1 can (16 oz.) **TACO BELL® HOME ORIGINALS®** Refried Beans
- 1 cup finely chopped red and green bell peppers
- ½ lb. (8 oz.) **VELVEETA** Pepper Jack Pasteurized Prepared Cheese Product, sliced
- 1 cup shredded lettuce
- ½ cup **TACO BELL® HOME ORIGINALS®** Thick 'N Chunky Salsa

PREHEAT oven to 350°F. Spread tostada shells with beans; top evenly with bell peppers and **VELVEETA**.

BAKE 5 to 7 min. or until **VELVEETA** is melted.

TOP with lettuce and salsa.

Makes 8 servings, 1 tostada each.

VARIATION-CRISPY BEEF TOSTADAS:

Omit refried beans. Brown 1 lb. lean ground beef in medium skillet; drain. Return to skillet. Add 1 pkg. (1¼ oz.) TACO BELL® HOME ORIGINALS® Taco Seasoning Mix; prepare as directed on package. Spoon meat mixture evenly onto tostada shells. Top with peppers and VELVEETA. Continue as directed.

SERVING SUGGESTION:

Serve with a tossed green salad drizzled with KRAFT Light Ranch Reduced Fat Dressing.

TACO BELL® and HOME ORIGINALS® are trademarks owned and licensed by Taco Bell Corp.

Chimichangas

Prep: 15 min. ● Total: 55 min. (incl. refrigerating)

- 1 lb. ground beef
- ½ cup finely chopped onions
- 2 cloves garlic, minced
- 1 tsp. dried oregano leaves
- 1 tsp. crushed red pepper
- 6 oz. **VELVEETA** Pasteurized Prepared Cheese Product, cut into 8 slices
- 8 **TACO BELL® HOME ORIGINALS®** Flour Tortillas
- 2 cups oil
- ¼ cup **BREAKSTONE'S** or **KNUDSEN** Sour Cream
- ¼ cup finely chopped fresh cilantro

BROWN meat in large skillet on medium-high heat; drain. Add onions, garlic, oregano and crushed red pepper; mix well. Cook until onions are tender, stirring occasionally; drain.

PLACE ¼ cup of the meat mixture and 1 **VELVEETA** slice in the center of each tortilla. Fold in all sides of tortillas to completely enclose filling; secure with wooden toothpicks. Place in single layer on baking sheet; cover. Refrigerate 20 min.

HEAT oil in large saucepan on medium-high heat. Add tortilla pouches, 2 at a time; cook 5 min. or until golden brown. Drain. Remove toothpicks. Top each serving with 1 Tbsp. *each* of the sour cream and cilantro.

Makes 4 servings, 2 chimichangas each.

VARIATION:

Save 110 calories and 14 g total fat per serving by substituting 1 lb. potatoes, cooked and cubed, for the browned ground beef and by using VELVEETA Made With 2% Milk Reduced Fat Pasteurized Prepared Process Cheese Product and BREAKSTONE'S Reduced Fat or KNUDSEN Light Sour Cream. To prepare, cook and stir onions with seasonings in large skillet 3 min. or until crisp-tender. Add potatoes; cook 3 to 5 min. or until potatoes are heated through, stirring frequently. Spoon onto tortillas and continue as directed.

Speedy Spicy Quesadillas

Prep: 5 min. • Total: 8 min.

½ lb. (8 oz.) Mild **VELVEETA** Mexican Pasteurized Prepared Cheese Product with Jalapeño Peppers, cut into 8 slices

8 flour tortillas (6 inch)

PLACE 1 **VELVEETA** slice on each tortilla. Fold tortillas in half. Place 2 tortillas on microwaveable plate.

MICROWAVE on HIGH 30 to 45 sec. or until **VELVEETA** is melted. Repeat with remaining tortillas.

CUT each quesadilla in half. Serve immediately.

Makes 8 servings, 2 quesadilla halves each.

SUBSTITUTE:

Prepare as directed, using VELVEETA Made With 2% Milk Reduced Fat Pasteurized Prepared Cheese Product.

FOOD FACTS:

Flour tortillas, often used as soft taco shells, come in many colors and sizes. Look for them in the dairy case or grocery aisle of the supermarket. You'll also find them seasoned with herbs, tomatoes, spinach or sesame seeds.

JAZZ IT UP:

Garnish with chopped fresh tomatoes and green onions.

Cheesy Scramblin' Pizza

Prep: 10 min. • Bake: 10 min.

- 6 eggs
- ¼ cup milk
- ¼ cup sliced green onions
- 1 small tomato, chopped
- 1 Italian pizza crust (12 inch)
- ½ lb. (8 oz.) **VELVEETA** Pasteurized Prepared Cheese Product, cut into ½-inch cubes
- 6 slices **OSCAR MAYER** Ready to Serve Bacon, cut into 1-inch pieces

PREHEAT oven to 450°F. Beat eggs, milk, onions and tomatoes with wire whisk until well blended. Pour into medium skillet sprayed with nonstick cooking spray. Cook on medium-low heat until eggs are set, stirring occasionally.

PLACE pizza crust on baking sheet; top with egg mixture and **VELVEETA**. Sprinkle with bacon.

BAKE 10 min. or until **VELVEETA** is melted. Cut into wedges to serve.

Makes 8 servings, 1 wedge each.

SERVING SUGGESTION:

For a delightful brunch idea, serve this Cheesy Scramblin' Pizza with a seasonal fresh fruit salad.

VARIATION:

Prepare as directed substituting 6 English muffins, split, toasted, for the pizza crust. Makes 12 servings.

SUBSTITUTE:

Substitute ½ lb. (8 oz.) VELVEETA Mild Mexican Pasteurized Prepared Cheese Product with Jalapeño Peppers for the VELVEETA Pasteurized Prepared Cheese Product.

Ultimate VELVEETA Nachos

Prep: 10 min. ● Total: 10 min.

- 1 lb. extra-lean ground beef
- 7 cups (6 oz.) tortilla chips
- ½ lb. (8 oz.) **VELVEETA** Pasteurized Prepared Cheese Product, cut into ½-inch cubes
- 1 cup shredded lettuce
- ½ cup chopped tomatoes
- ¼ cup sliced black olives
- ⅓ cup **BREAKSTONE'S** or **KNUDSEN** Sour Cream

BROWN meat; drain.

ARRANGE chips on microwaveable platter; top evenly with **VELVEETA**. Microwave on HIGH 2 min. or until **VELVEETA** is melted.

TOP with meat and remaining ingredients.

Makes 6 servings.

HEALTHY LIVING:

By preparing this dish with extra-lean ground beef (95% fat) instead of ground beef (80% fat), you will save 5g fat and 40 calories per serving.

JAZZ IT UP:

Season the meat with taco seasoning before spooning over the chips. Just brown the meat as directed. Then, add 1 pkg. (1¼ oz.) TACO BELL® HOME ORIGINALS® Taco Seasoning Mix and prepare as directed on package.

TACO BELL® and HOME ORIGINALS® are trademarks owned and licensed by Taco Bell Corp.

Cheesy Potato Skins

Prep: 15 min. ● Total: 35 min.

- 4 large baked potatoes
- 2 Tbsp. butter or margarine, melted
- ¼ lb. (4 oz.) **VELVEETA** Pasteurized Prepared Cheese Product, cut into ½-inch cubes
- 2 Tbsp. chopped red bell peppers
- 2 slices **OSCAR MAYER** Bacon, crisply cooked, crumbled
- 1 Tbsp. sliced green onions

PREHEAT oven to 450°F. Cut potatoes in half lengthwise; scoop out centers, leaving ¼-inch-thick shells. (Refrigerate removed potato centers for another use.) Cut shells crosswise in half. Place, skin-sides down, on baking sheet; brush with butter.

BAKE 20 to 25 min. or until crisp and golden brown.

FILL shells evenly with **VELVEETA**; continue baking until **VELVEETA** begins to melt. Top with remaining ingredients.

Makes 16 servings, 1 appetizer each.

SUBSTITUTE:

Substitute green bell peppers for the red bell peppers.

HOW TO BAKE POTATOES:

Russet potatoes are the best for baking. Scrub potatoes well, blot dry and rub the skin with a little oil and salt. Prick the skin of the potatoes with a fork so steam can escape. Stand them on end in a muffin tin. Bake at 425°F for 45 min. to 1 hour or until tender.

HOW TO USE GREEN ONIONS:

Green onions add a deliciously mild onion flavor to foods. To use them, trim off the roots and remove any wilted, brown or damaged tops, then slice and use as much of the white end and green shoot as you like.

Macaroni and Cheese Dijon

Prep: 20 min. • Total: 45 min.

1¼ cups milk

½ lb. (8 oz.) **VELVEETA** Pasteurized Prepared Cheese Product, cut into ½-inch cubes

2 Tbsp. **GREY POUPON** Dijon Mustard

6 slices **OSCAR MAYER** Bacon, cooked, drained and crumbled

⅓ cup green onion slices

⅛ tsp. ground red pepper (cayenne)

3½ cups tri-colored rotini pasta, cooked, drained

½ cup French fried onion rings

PREHEAT oven to 350°F. Mix milk, **VELVEETA** and mustard in medium saucepan; cook on low heat until **VELVEETA** is completely melted and mixture is well blended, stirring occasionally. Add bacon, green onions and pepper; mix lightly. Remove from heat. Add to pasta in large bowl; toss to coat.

SPOON into greased 2-qt. casserole dish; cover.

BAKE 15 to 20 min. or until heated through. Uncover; stir. Top with onion rings. Bake, uncovered, an additional 5 min. Let stand 10 min. before serving.

Makes 6 servings, 1 cup each.

MAKE IT EASY:

For easy crumbled bacon, use kitchen scissors to snip raw bacon into ½-inch pieces. Let pieces fall right into skillet, then cook until crisp and drain on paper towels.

VELVEETA Baked Spaghetti Squares

Prep: 15 min. ● Total: 50 min.

- 4 eggs
- ¼ cup milk
- 1 pkg. (16 oz.) spaghetti, cooked, drained
- 1 green bell pepper, chopped
- 1 can (7 oz.) mushroom pieces and stems, drained
- 1 small onion, chopped
- ½ lb. (8 oz.) **VELVEETA** Pasteurized Prepared Cheese Product, cut into ½-inch cubes
- ½ cup **KRAFT** 100% Grated Parmesan Cheese
- 1 jar (26 oz.) spaghetti sauce, warmed

PREHEAT oven to 350°F. Beat eggs and milk in large bowl with wire whisk until well blended. Add spaghetti, peppers, mushrooms, onions, **VELVEETA** and Parmesan cheese.

SPOON into 13×9-inch baking dish sprayed with cooking spray; press into dish with back of spoon.

BAKE 30 to 35 min. or until heated through. Cut into 8 squares. Serve each square topped with about ¼ cup of the spaghetti sauce.

Makes 8 servings.

VARIATION:

Prepare as directed, using VELVEETA Made with 2% Milk Reduced Fat Pasteurized Prepared Cheese Product and substituting 1 cup cholesterol-free egg product for the 4 eggs.

Cheesy Chicken & Broccoli Bake

Prep: 10 min. ● Total: 40 min.

- 1 pkg. (6 oz.) **STOVE TOP** Stuffing Mix for Chicken
- 1½ lb. boneless, skinless chicken breasts, cut into 1-inch pieces
- 1 pkg. (16 oz.) frozen broccoli florets, thawed, drained
- 1 can (10¾ oz.) reduced-sodium condensed cream of chicken soup
- ½ lb. (8 oz.) **VELVEETA** Pasteurized Prepared Cheese Product, cut into ½-inch cubes

PREHEAT oven to 400°F. Prepare stuffing mix as directed on package.

MEANWHILE, combine remaining ingredients in 13×9-inch baking dish. Top with stuffing.

BAKE 30 min. or until chicken is cooked through.

Makes 6 servings.

SUBSTITUTE:

Substitute ¾ cup CHEEZ WHIZ Cheese Dip for the cubed VELVEETA.

VARIATION:

Prepare as directed, using VELVEETA Made With 2% Milk Reduced Fat Pasteurized Cheese Product.

VELVEETA Ultimate Macaroni & Cheese

Prep: 20 min. • Total: 20 min.

- 2 cups (8 oz.) elbow macaroni, uncooked
- ¾ lb. (12 oz.) **VELVEETA** Pasteurized Prepared Cheese Product, cut into ½-inch cubes
- ⅓ cup milk
- ⅛ tsp. black pepper

COOK macaroni as directed on package; drain well. Return to pan.

ADD remaining ingredients; mix well. Cook on low heat until **VELVEETA** is completely melted and mixture is well blended, stirring frequently.

Makes 4 servings, 1 cup each.

HEALTHY LIVING:

Save 70 calories and 10 grams of fat per serving by preparing with VELVEETA Made With 2% Milk Reduced Fat Pasteurized Prepared Cheese Product.

VARIATION:

Prepare as directed. Pour into 2-qt. casserole dish. Bake at 350°F for 25 min.

DRESSED-UP MAC 'N CHEESE:

Substitute bow-tie pasta or your favorite shaped pasta for the macaroni.

VELVEETA Double-Decker Nachos

Prep: 15 min. • Total: 15 min.

- 6 oz. tortilla chips (about 7 cups)
- 1 can (15 oz.) chili with beans
- ½ lb. (8 oz.) **VELVEETA** Pasteurized Prepared Cheese Product, cut into ½-inch cubes
- 1 medium tomato, finely chopped
- ¼ cup sliced green onions
- ⅓ cup **BREAKSTONE'S** or **KNUDSEN** Sour Cream

ARRANGE half of the chips on large microwaveable platter; top with layers of half *each* of the chili and **VELVEETA**. Repeat layers.

MICROWAVE on HIGH 3 to 5 min. or until **VELVEETA** is melted.

TOP with remaining ingredients.

Makes 6 servings.

SIZE-WISE:

Enjoy your favorite foods while keeping portion size in mind.

SUBSTITUTE:

Prepare as directed, using VELVEETA Mild Mexican Pasteurized Prepared Cheese Product with Jalapeño Peppers.